# TABLE OF
# CONTENTS

# ·DUMP·
## BREAKFAST

# BAKED PUMPKIN OATMEAL

MAKES 6 SERVINGS

2 cups milk

1 cup canned pumpkin

2 eggs

⅓ cup packed brown sugar

1 teaspoon vanilla

2 cups old-fashioned oats, toasted*

½ cup dried cranberries

1 teaspoon pumpkin pie spice

½ teaspoon salt

½ teaspoon baking powder

Maple syrup

Chopped pecans (optional)

*Spread oats on ungreased baking sheet. Bake about 10 minutes or until fragrant and lightly browned, stirring occasionally. Cool slightly.*

**1.** Preheat oven to 350°F. Spray 8-inch square baking dish with nonstick cooking spray.

**2.** Whisk milk, pumpkin, eggs, brown sugar and vanilla in large bowl until well blended. Stir in oats, cranberries, pumpkin pie spice, salt and baking powder until well blended. Pour into prepared dish.

**3.** Bake about 45 minutes or until oatmeal is set and knife inserted into center comes out almost clean. Serve warm with maple syrup and pecans, if desired.

# CRUSTLESS SALMON AND BROCCOLI QUICHE

MAKES 4 SERVINGS

- 3 eggs
- ¼ cup chopped green onions
- ¼ cup plain yogurt
- 2 teaspoons all-purpose flour
- 1 teaspoon dried basil
- ⅛ teaspoon salt
- ⅛ teaspoon black pepper
- ¾ cup frozen broccoli florets, thawed and drained

- 1 can (6 ounces) boneless skinless salmon, drained and flaked
- 2 tablespoons grated Parmesan cheese
- 1 plum tomato, thinly sliced
- ¼ cup fresh bread crumbs

**1.** Preheat oven to 375°F. Spray 1½-quart baking dish or 9-inch deep-dish pie plate with nonstick cooking spray.

**2.** Whisk eggs, green onions, yogurt, flour, basil, salt and pepper in medium bowl until well blended. Stir in broccoli, salmon and cheese. Spread evenly in prepared dish. Top with tomato slices and sprinkle with bread crumbs.

**3.** Bake 20 to 25 minutes or until knife inserted near center comes out clean. Let stand 5 minutes before serving.

# BLUEBERRY–ORANGE FRENCH TOAST CASSEROLE

MAKES 6 SERVINGS

½ cup sugar
½ cup milk
2 eggs
4 egg whites
1 tablespoon grated orange peel

½ teaspoon vanilla
6 slices whole wheat bread, cut into 1-inch pieces
1 cup fresh blueberries

**1.** Preheat oven to 350°F. Spray 8-inch square baking dish with nonstick cooking spray.

**2.** Whisk sugar, milk, eggs, egg whites, orange peel and vanilla in large bowl until well blended. Stir in bread and blueberries. Pour into prepared dish. Let stand 5 minutes.

**3.** Bake 40 to 45 minutes or until bread is browned and center is almost set. Let stand 5 minutes before serving.

# CHILE–CORN QUICHE

MAKES 6 SERVINGS

1 unbaked 9-inch pie crust

1 can (8¾ ounces) whole kernel corn, drained *or* 1 cup thawed frozen corn

1 can (4 ounces) diced mild green chiles, drained

¼ cup thinly sliced green onions

1 cup (4 ounces) shredded Monterey Jack cheese

1½ cups half-and-half

3 eggs

½ teaspoon salt

½ teaspoon ground cumin

**1.** Preheat oven to 450°F. Bake pie crust according to package directions for empty crust. Let cool. *Reduce oven temperature to 375°F.*

**2.** Combine corn, chiles and green onions in medium bowl. Spoon into crust; top with cheese. Whisk half-and-half, eggs, salt and cumin in same bowl. Pour over cheese.

**3.** Bake 35 to 45 minutes or until filling is puffed and knife inserted into center comes out clean. Let stand 10 minutes before serving.

# WARM APPLE–BLUEBERRY CRISP

MAKES 6 SERVINGS

6   apples, peeled and sliced

2   cups frozen blueberries

½   cup packed brown sugar, divided

¼   cup orange juice

½   cup biscuit baking mix

½   cup old-fashioned oats

¼   cup (½ stick) cold butter, cut into small pieces

¼   teaspoon ground cinnamon

¼   teaspoon ground ginger

**1.** Preheat oven to 375°F. Spray 9-inch square baking pan with nonstick cooking spray.

**2.** Combine apples, blueberries, ¼ cup brown sugar and orange juice in prepared pan; toss to coat. Spread in even layer.

**3.** Combine baking mix, oats, remaining ¼ cup brown sugar, butter, cinnamon and ginger in small bowl; mix with fingertips until coarse crumbs form. Sprinkle over fruit mixture.

**4.** Bake 45 minutes or until apples are tender and topping is golden brown.

# OVERNIGHT HAM AND CHEESE BREAD PUDDING

MAKES 8 SERVINGS

3 tablespoons butter, softened

1 small loaf (8 ounces) sourdough, country French or Italian bread, cut into 1-inch cubes

8 ounces ham or smoked ham, cubed

1 cup (4 ounces) shredded Cheddar cheese

2 cups milk

3 eggs

1 teaspoon ground mustard

½ teaspoon salt

⅛ teaspoon white pepper

**1.** Generously grease 11×7-inch baking dish with butter. Spread bread cubes in prepared dish; top with ham and sprinkle with cheese.

**2.** Whisk milk, eggs, mustard, salt and pepper in medium bowl. Pour evenly over bread mixture. Cover and refrigerate at least 6 hours or overnight.

**3.** Preheat oven to 350°F. Bake bread pudding, uncovered, 45 to 50 minutes or until puffed and golden brown and knife inserted into center comes out clean.

# MAKE-AHEAD CINNAMON FRENCH TOAST CASSEROLE

MAKES 6 TO 8 SERVINGS

1 loaf (16 ounces) French bread, cut into 1½-inch slices

6 to 8 baking apples, such as Granny Smith, McIntosh or Cortland, peeled and sliced

3½ cups milk

9 eggs

1½ cups sugar, divided

1 tablespoon vanilla

½ teaspoon salt

1 teaspoon ground cinnamon

½ teaspoon ground nutmeg

**1.** Spray 13×9-inch baking dish with nonstick cooking spray. Arrange bread slices in single layer in prepared dish; top with apple slices.

**2.** Whisk milk, eggs, 1 cup sugar, vanilla and salt in large bowl until well blended. Pour over apples and bread.

**3.** Combine remaining ½ cup granulated sugar, cinnamon and nutmeg in small bowl; sprinkle over casserole. Cover and refrigerate overnight.

**4.** Preheat oven to 350°F. Bake casserole, uncovered, 1 hour or until set.

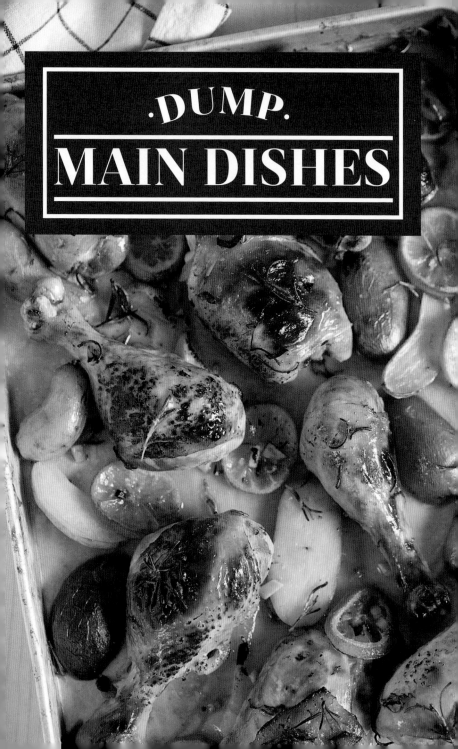

# ·DUMP·
# MAIN DISHES

# HONEY-LEMON GARLIC CHICKEN

MAKES 4 SERVINGS

2 lemons, divided

2 tablespoons butter, melted

2 tablespoons honey

3 cloves garlic, chopped

2 sprigs fresh rosemary, leaves removed from stems

1 teaspoon coarse salt

½ teaspoon black pepper

3 pounds chicken (4 bone-in skin-on chicken thighs and 4 drumsticks)

1¼ pounds potatoes, cut into halves or quarters

**1.** Preheat oven to 375°F. Grate peel and squeeze juice from one lemon. Cut remaining lemon into slices.

**2.** Combine lemon peel, lemon juice, butter, honey, garlic, rosemary leaves, salt and pepper in medium bowl; mix well. Combine chicken, potatoes and lemon slices in large bowl. Pour butter mixture over chicken and potatoes; toss to coat. Spread in single layer on large rimmed baking sheet or in shallow roasting pan.

**3.** Bake about 1 hour or until potatoes are tender and chicken is cooked through (165°F). Cover loosely with foil if chicken skin is browning too quickly.

# SPINACH-CHEESE PASTA CASSEROLE

MAKES 6 TO 8 SERVINGS

2 eggs

1 jar (26 ounces) marinara sauce

1 package (10 ounces) frozen chopped spinach, thawed and squeezed dry

8 ounces uncooked shell pasta, cooked according to package directions

1 cup ricotta cheese

1 teaspoon salt

1 cup (4 ounces) shredded mozzarella cheese

¼ cup grated Parmesan cheese

**1.** Preheat oven to 350°F. Spray 1½-quart baking dish with nonstick cooking spray.

**2.** Whisk eggs in large bowl until blended; stir in marinara sauce, spinach, pasta, ricotta cheese and salt until well blended. Pour into prepared dish. Sprinkle evenly with mozzarella and Parmesan cheeses.

**3.** Cover and bake 30 minutes. Remove cover; bake 15 minutes or until hot and bubbly.

# CHICKEN BROCCOLI RICE CASSEROLE

## MAKES 4 TO 6 SERVINGS

3 cups cooked long grain rice

1 pound chopped cooked chicken

1½ pounds broccoli, cut into bite-size pieces

2 cans (10¾ ounces each) condensed cream of celery soup, undiluted

¾ cup mayonnaise

½ cup milk

2 teaspoons curry powder

3 cups (12 ounces) shredded sharp Cheddar cheese

**1.** Preheat oven to 350°F. Spray 13×9-inch baking dish with nonstick cooking spray.

**2.** Spread rice evenly in prepared dish. Top with chicken and broccoli. Mix soup, mayonnaise, milk and curry powder in medium bowl; pour over chicken and broccoli. Top with cheese. Cover loosely with foil.

**3.** Bake 45 minutes or until cheese is melted, broccoli is tender and casserole is heated through.

# CAJUN-STYLE BEEF AND BEANS

MAKES 6 SERVINGS

1 pound 95% lean ground beef

¾ cup chopped onion

2½ cups cooked brown rice

1 can (about 15 ounces) kidney beans, rinsed and drained

1 can (about 14 ounces) stewed tomatoes

2 teaspoons Cajun seasoning, or to taste*

¾ cup (3 ounces) shredded reduced-fat Cheddar cheese

*Depending on the brand, Cajun seasoning may be high in sodium. Taste and adjust the seasoning if necessary.*

1. Preheat oven to 350°F.

2. Brown beef in large ovenproof skillet or Dutch oven over medium-high heat 6 to 8 minutes, stirring to break up meat. Drain fat. Add onion; cook and stir 2 minutes or until translucent. Stir in rice, beans, tomatoes and Cajun seasoning.

3. Cover and bake 25 to 30 minutes, stirring once. Sprinkle with cheese. Cover and let stand 5 minutes before serving.

TIP: To make your own Cajun seasoning, combine 5 tablespoons ground red pepper, 3 tablespoons black pepper, 3 tablespoons onion powder, 3 tablespoons garlic powder, 3 tablespoons chili powder, 1 tablespoon dried thyme, 1 tablespoon dried basil and 1 tablespoon ground bay leaf in a medium bowl until the spices are well combined. If desired, stir in ½ cup salt. Store in a tightly sealed container.

# COUNTRY CHICKEN AND BISCUITS

MAKES 4 SERVINGS

1   can (10.75 oz.) condensed cream of celery soup

⅓  cup milk or water

4   boneless, skinless chicken breast halves, cooked and cut into bite-sized pieces

1   can (14.5 oz.) Del Monte® Cut Green Beans, drained

Black pepper (optional)

1   can (11 oz.) refrigerated biscuits

**1.** Preheat oven to 375°F.

**2.** Combine soup and milk in large bowl. Gently stir in chicken and green beans; season with pepper, if desired. Spoon into 11×7-inch or 2-quart baking dish.

**3.** Cover with foil and bake at 375°F 20 to 25 minutes or until hot.

**4.** Separate biscuit dough into individual biscuits. Immediately arrange biscuits over hot mixture. Bake about 15 minutes or until biscuits are golden brown and baked through.

**MICROWAVE DIRECTIONS:** To prepare this dish even faster, use a microwavable baking dish in step 2. Cover with plastic wrap; slit to vent. Microwave on HIGH 8 to 10 minutes or until heated through, rotating dish once. Continue as directed in step 4.

# HEARTY POTATO AND SAUSAGE BAKE

MAKES 4 TO 6 SERVINGS

1 pound new red potatoes, cut into halves or quarters

1 onion, sliced

½ pound carrots, cut into 3-inch sticks or baby carrots

2 tablespoons butter, melted

1 teaspoon salt

1 teaspoon garlic powder

½ teaspoon dried thyme

½ teaspoon black pepper

1 pound cooked chicken sausage or turkey sausage, cut into ¼-inch slices

**1.** Preheat oven to 400°F. Spray 13×9-inch baking dish with nonstick cooking spray.

**2.** Combine potatoes, onion, carrots, butter, salt, garlic powder, thyme and pepper in large bowl; toss to coat. Spread in prepared dish.

**3.** Bake 30 minutes. Stir in sausage. Bake 15 to 20 minutes or until potatoes are tender and golden brown.

# FORTY-CLOVE CHICKEN

MAKES 4 TO 6 SERVINGS

¼ cup olive oil

1 (3-pound) frying chicken, cut into serving pieces

40 cloves garlic (about 2 heads), peeled

½ cup dry white wine

¼ cup dry vermouth

4 stalks celery, thickly sliced

2 tablespoons finely chopped fresh parsley

2 teaspoons dried basil

1 teaspoon dried oregano, crushed

Pinch of red pepper flakes

Grated peel and juice of 1 lemon

Salt and black pepper

**1.** Preheat oven to 375°F.

**2.** Heat oil in Dutch oven. Add chicken; cook until browned on all sides. Stir in garlic, wine, vermouth, celery, parsley, basil, oregano and red pepper flakes. Sprinkle lemon peel over chicken; pour lemon juice over top of chicken. Season with salt and black pepper.

**3.** Cover and bake 40 minutes. Remove cover; bake 15 minutes or until chicken is tender and juices run clear.

# ROAST CHICKEN AND POTATOES CATALAN

MAKES 4 SERVINGS

2   tablespoons olive oil

2   tablespoons lemon juice

1   teaspoon dried thyme

½   teaspoon salt

¼   teaspoon ground red pepper

¼   teaspoon ground saffron *or* ½ teaspoon turmeric

2   large baking potatoes (about 1½ pounds), cut into 1½-inch chunks

4   skinless bone-in chicken breast halves (about 2 pounds)

1   cup sliced red bell pepper

1   cup frozen peas, thawed

**1.** Preheat oven to 400°F. Spray large shallow roasting pan or 15×10-inch jelly-roll pan with nonstick cooking spray.

**2.** Combine oil, lemon juice, thyme, salt, ground red pepper and saffron in large bowl; mix well. Add potatoes; toss to coat. Arrange potatoes in single layer around edges of pan. Place chicken in center of pan; drizzle remaining oil mixture in bowl over chicken.

**3.** Bake 20 minutes. Stir potatoes and add bell pepper to pan; baste chicken with pan juices. Bake 20 minutes or until chicken is no longer pink in center, juices run clear and potatoes are browned. Sprinkle peas over potatoes; bake 5 minutes or until heated through.

# CHICKEN TETRAZZINI CASSEROLE

MAKES 4 SERVINGS

1 can (10¾ ounces) condensed cream of mushroom soup, undiluted

¼ cup half-and-half

3 tablespoons dry sherry

½ teaspoon salt

⅛ to ¼ teaspoon red pepper flakes

2 cups chopped cooked chicken

8 ounces uncooked vermicelli pasta, broken in half and cooked according to package directions

1 cup frozen peas

½ cup grated Parmesan cheese

1 cup panko bread crumbs or coarse fresh bread crumbs

2 tablespoons butter, melted

**1.** Preheat oven to 375°F. Spray 8-inch square baking dish with nonstick cooking spray.

**2.** Combine soup, half-and-half, sherry, salt and red pepper flakes in large bowl. Stir in chicken, pasta, peas and cheese; stir until well coated. Pour into prepared dish. Combine bread crumbs and butter in small bowl; sprinkle evenly over casserole.

**3.** Bake 25 to 30 minutes or until heated through and crumbs are golden brown.

# BAKED MOSTACCIOLI

MAKES 8 SERVINGS

1 container (15 ounces) part-skim ricotta cheese

2 eggs

¼ cup grated Parmesan cheese

½ teaspoon garlic powder

½ teaspoon dried Italian seasoning

½ teaspoon salt

¼ teaspoon black pepper

1 package (16 ounces) uncooked mostaccioli or penne pasta, cooked according to package directions

1 jar (26 ounces) pasta sauce

1½ cups (6 ounces) shredded mozzarella cheese

**1.** Preheat oven to 350°F. Spray 13×9-inch baking dish with nonstick cooking spray.

**2.** Combine ricotta cheese, eggs, Parmesan cheese, garlic powder, Italian seasoning, salt and pepper in medium bowl; mix well.

**3.** Place half of pasta and half of sauce in prepared dish. Spread ricotta mixture evenly over pasta; top with remaining pasta, sauce, ricotta mixture and mozzarella cheese.

**4.** Bake 30 minutes or until hot and bubbly.

# TUNA–MACARONI CASSEROLE

MAKES 6 SERVINGS

1   cup mayonnaise

1   cup (4 ounces) shredded Swiss cheese

½   cup milk

¼   cup chopped onion

¼   cup chopped red bell pepper

⅛   teaspoon black pepper

2   cans (about 6 ounces each) tuna, drained and flaked

1   package (about 10 ounces) frozen peas

2   cups uncooked shell pasta or elbow macaroni, cooked according to package directions

½   cup dry bread crumbs

2   tablespoons melted butter

**1.** Preheat oven to 350°F.

**2.** Combine mayonnaise, cheese, milk, onion, bell pepper and black pepper in large bowl. Stir in tuna, peas and pasta. Pour into 2-quart baking dish.

**3.** Mix bread crumbs and butter in small bowl; sprinkle over top of casserole. Bake 30 to 40 minutes or until heated through.

# POTATO AND MEATBALL CASSEROLE

MAKES 8 SERVINGS

6   potatoes, thinly sliced
6 to 8 carrots, thinly sliced
2   onions, thinly sliced
    Salt and black pepper

1   can (46 ounces) tomato juice
1   can (10 ounces) diced tomatoes and green chiles
16  frozen fully cooked meatballs

1. Preheat oven to 375°F. Spray 13×9-inch baking pan with nonstick cooking spray.

2. Arrange potatoes, carrots and onions in prepared pan. Season with salt and pepper. Pour tomato juice and chopped tomatoes over vegetables.

3. Bake 1½ hours or until vegetables are tender. Top with meatballs; bake 15 minutes or until browned.

# BAKED PASTA AND CHEESE SUPREME

MAKES 4 SERVINGS

12 slices bacon, diced

½ medium onion, chopped

2 cloves garlic, minced

2 teaspoons dried oregano, divided

1 can (8 ounces) tomato sauce

1 teaspoon hot pepper sauce (optional)

8 ounces uncooked fusilli pasta or other corkscrew-shaped pasta, cooked according to package directions

1½ cups (6 ounces) shredded Cheddar or Colby cheese

½ cup fresh bread crumbs or panko bread crumbs

1 tablespoon butter, melted

**1.** Preheat oven to 400°F. Cook bacon in large ovenproof skillet over medium heat until crisp. Drain on paper towels.

**2.** Add onion, garlic and 1 teaspoon oregano to skillet; cook and stir 3 minutes or until onion is translucent. Stir in tomato sauce and hot pepper sauce, if desired. Add pasta and cheese; stir to coat.

**3.** Combine bacon, bread crumbs, remaining 1 teaspoon oregano and butter in small bowl; sprinkle over pasta mixture. Bake 10 to 15 minutes or until hot and bubbly.

# .DUMP.
# SIDE DISHES

# SKILLET ROASTED ROOT VEGETABLES

MAKES 4 SERVINGS

1 sweet potato, peeled, cut in half lengthwise and cut crosswise into ½-inch slices

1 large red onion, cut into 1-inch wedges

2 parsnips, cut diagonally into 1-inch slices

2 carrots, cut diagonally into 1-inch slices

1 turnip, peeled, cut in half and then cut into ½-inch slices

2½ tablespoons olive oil

1½ tablespoons honey

1½ tablespoons balsamic vinegar

1 teaspoon coarse salt

1 teaspoon dried thyme

¼ teaspoon ground red pepper

¼ teaspoon black pepper

1. Preheat oven to 400°F.

2. Combine all ingredients in large bowl; toss to coat. Spread vegetables in single layer in large (12-inch) cast iron skillet.

3. Roast 1 hour or until vegetables are tender, stirring once halfway through cooking time.

# HASH BROWN CASSEROLE WITH BACON

MAKES ABOUT 8 SERVINGS

1 package (32 ounces) refrigerated diced potatoes, thawed

1 container (16 ounces) sour cream

1 can (10¾ ounces) condensed cream of chicken soup, undiluted

1½ cups (6 ounces) shredded sharp Cheddar cheese

¾ cup thinly sliced green onions

4 slices bacon, crisp-cooked and crumbled

2 teaspoons hot pepper sauce

¼ teaspoon garlic salt

1. Preheat oven to 350°F. Spray 13×9-inch baking pan with nonstick cooking spray.

2. Combine potatoes, sour cream, soup, cheese, green onions, bacon, hot pepper sauce and garlic salt in large bowl. Spoon evenly into prepared pan.

3. Bake 55 to 60 minutes or until potatoes are tender and cooked through. Stir before serving.

# OATMEAL DROP BISCUITS

MAKES ABOUT 16 BISCUITS

1½ cups all-purpose flour

½ cup quick oats

1 tablespoon baking powder

2 teaspoons sugar

½ teaspoon salt

½ teaspoon grated orange peel

6 tablespoons cold butter, cut into small pieces

¾ cup milk

1. Preheat oven to 450°F.

2. Combine flour, oats, baking powder, sugar, salt and orange peel in large bowl. Cut in butter with pastry blender or fingers until mixture resembles coarse crumbs. Stir in milk just until moistened. Drop dough by rounded tablespoonfuls 2 inches apart onto ungreased baking sheets.

3. Bake 10 to 12 minutes until golden brown on bottoms. Serve immediately.

# FOUR-CHEESE MAC AND CHEESE

MAKES 8 SERVINGS

4 cups milk

2 cups (8 ounces) shredded sharp Cheddar cheese

2 cups (8 ounces) shredded American cheese

2 cups (8 ounces) shredded Muenster cheese

1 cup (4 ounces) shredded mozzarella cheese

Salt and black pepper

1 package (16 ounces) uncooked elbow macaroni, cooked according to package directions

1. Preheat oven to 350°F.

2. Bring milk to a simmer in large saucepan over medium heat. Reduce heat to low. Gradually add cheeses, stirring constantly. Cook and stir 5 minutes or until smooth. Season with salt and pepper to taste.

3. Place macaroni in 4-quart baking dish. Pour cheese sauce over macaroni; stir until well blended. Bake 50 to 60 minutes or until bubbly and heated through.

TIP: For a crunchy topping, combine 1 cup dry bread crumbs, panko or crushed round butter crackers and 2 tablespoons melted butter in small bowl. Sprinkle evenly over casserole. Cover with foil and bake as directed above, removing foil during last 15 minutes of baking.

# WHOLE WHEAT KUGEL

MAKES 9 SIDE-DISH OR 6 MAIN-DISH SERVINGS

1 container (15 ounces) ricotta cheese

1 cup sour cream

¼ cup sugar

¼ teaspoon ground cinnamon, plus additional for garnish

½ teaspoon salt

3 eggs

8 ounces uncooked whole wheat linguine, broken into 3-inch pieces and cooked according to package directions

1. Preheat oven to 350°F. Grease 8-inch square baking dish.

2. Combine ricotta, sour cream, sugar, ¼ teaspoon cinnamon and salt in large bowl. Add eggs; beat until smooth. Add linguine; mix well. Pour into prepared dish.

3. Bake 45 to 50 minutes or until firm and lightly browned on top. Sprinkle with additional cinnamon just before serving, if desired.

# CHEDDAR BROCCOLI CASSEROLE

## MAKES 8 SERVINGS

1 can (10¾ ounces) condensed cream of mushroom soup, undiluted

1 cup (4 ounces) shredded Cheddar cheese

2 eggs

¼ cup plain Greek yogurt

1 teaspoon salt

1 can (5 ounces) sliced water chestnuts, drained

½ cup chopped onion

2 packages (9 ounces each) frozen chopped broccoli, thawed

8 round butter crackers, crushed

2 teaspoons butter, melted

**1.** Preheat oven to 350°F. Spray 2-quart baking dish with nonstick cooking spray.

**2.** Combine soup, cheese, eggs, yogurt and salt in large bowl; mix well. Stir in water chestnuts and onion. Fold in broccoli. Pour into prepared dish.

**3.** Bake 30 minutes. Combine crackers and butter in small bowl; sprinkle evenly over casserole. Bake 5 minutes or until lightly browned. Let stand 10 minutes before serving.

# POTATO NUGGET CASSEROLE

MAKES 10 SERVINGS

2 pounds frozen potato nuggets

1 can (10¾ ounces) condensed cream of celery soup, undiluted

1 can (10¾ ounces) condensed cream of mushroom soup, undiluted

1 can (10¾ ounces) condensed Cheddar cheese soup, undiluted

1 can (about 5 ounces) evaporated milk

2 cups (8 ounces) shredded mozzarella cheese

2 cups (8 ounces) shredded Cheddar cheese

1. Preheat oven to 350°F. Spread potato nuggets in 13×9-inch baking dish.

2. Combine soups and evaporated milk in large saucepan; bring to a boil, stirring occasionally. Pour over potatoes and stir until well blended.

3. Bake 45 minutes. Sprinkle mozzarella and Cheddar cheeses evenly over casserole. Bake 5 minutes or until cheeses are melted.

# PARMESAN PEPPERCORN DROP BISCUITS

MAKES 12 BISCUITS

2 cups all-purpose flour

⅓ cup finely grated Parmesan cheese

1 tablespoon baking powder

1 teaspoon black pepper

½ teaspoon salt

6 tablespoons (¾ stick) cold butter, cut into small pieces

1 cup buttermilk

1. Preheat oven to 425°F. Line baking sheet with parchment paper.

2. Combine flour, Parmesan cheese, baking powder, pepper and salt in large bowl. Cut in butter using pastry blender or fingers until mixture resembles coarse crumbs. Stir in buttermilk just until moistened. Drop dough by ¼ cupfuls onto prepared baking sheet.

3. Bake 12 minutes or until tops of biscuits are golden brown. Let stand 5 minutes before serving.

# PASTA AND WHITE BEAN CASSEROLE

MAKES 6 SERVINGS

1 tablespoon olive oil

½ cup chopped onion

2 cloves garlic, minced

2 cans (about 15 ounces each) cannellini beans, rinsed and drained

3 cups cooked small shell pasta

1 can (8 ounces) tomato sauce

1½ teaspoons dried Italian seasoning

½ teaspoon salt

½ teaspoon black pepper

1 cup (4 ounces) shredded Italian cheese blend

2 tablespoons finely chopped fresh Italian parsley

1. Preheat oven to 350°F. Spray 2-quart baking dish with nonstick cooking spray.

2. Heat oil in large skillet over medium-high heat. Add onion and garlic; cook and stir 4 minutes or until onion is tender. Add beans, pasta, tomato sauce, Italian seasoning, salt and pepper; mix well. Pour into prepared dish; sprinkle with cheese.

3. Bake 20 minutes or until cheese is melted. Sprinkle with parsley just before serving.

# PARTY POTATOES

1 package (32 ounces) Southern-style hash browns

2 cans (10¾ ounces each) condensed cream of potato soup, undiluted

2 cups (16 ounces) sour cream

2 cups (8 ounces) shredded Cheddar cheese

¾ cup finely chopped red onion

¼ cup (½ stick) butter, cut into pieces

Parmesan cheese (optional)

1. Preheat oven to 350°F. Spray 13×9-inch baking dish with nonstick cooking spray.

2. Combine hash browns, soup, sour cream, Cheddar cheese and onion in large bowl. Pour into prepared dish and pat into even layer. Dot with butter; sprinkle with Parmesan cheese, if desired.

3. Cover with foil; bake 50 minutes. Remove foil; bake 20 minutes or until browned.

# .ONE-BOWL.
# CHOCOLATE
# DESSERTS

# TRIPLE-CHOCOLATE PUDDING CAKE

## MAKES 8 SERVINGS

1 cup biscuit baking mix

½ cup sugar

¼ cup unsweetened cocoa powder

¾ cup milk, divided

⅓ cup butter, softened

¾ cup hot fudge topping, divided

1 teaspoon vanilla

1 cup semisweet chocolate chips, divided

¾ cup coffee or hot water

Fresh raspberries or whipped cream (optional)

1. Preheat oven to 350°F. Spray 8-inch square baking pan with nonstick cooking spray.

2. Combine baking mix, sugar and cocoa in medium bowl. Whisk in ½ cup milk, butter, ¼ cup hot fudge topping and vanilla until well blended. Stir in ½ cup chocolate chips. Pour batter into prepared pan.

3. Combine remaining ¼ cup milk, ½ cup hot fudge topping and coffee in same bowl; stir until well blended. Pour over batter in pan. *Do not stir.* Sprinkle remaining ½ cup chocolate chips over top.

4. Bake 45 to 50 minutes or until set. Cool in pan 15 minutes on wire rack. Spoon into dessert dishes. Garnish with raspberries.

# APRICOT DOUBLE CHIP DUMP CAKE

MAKES 9 SERVINGS

2 cups apricot preserves or jam

½ cup semisweet chocolate chips

½ cup white chocolate chips

1 package (about 15 ounces) yellow cake mix

½ cup (1 stick) butter, cut into thin slices

⅓ cup water

**1.** Preheat oven to 350°F. Spray 9-inch square baking pan with nonstick cooking spray.

**2.** Spread preserves in prepared pan. Sprinkle with half of semisweet chips and half of white chips. Top evenly with cake mix. Top with butter in single layer, covering cake mix as much as possible. Drizzle water over top. Sprinkle with remaining semisweet and white chips.

**3.** Bake 50 to 55 minutes or until toothpick inserted into center comes out clean. Cool at least 15 minutes before serving.

# S'MORES DUMP CAKE

MAKES 12 TO 16 SERVINGS

1 package (about 15 ounces) milk chocolate cake mix

1 package (4-serving size) chocolate instant pudding and pie filling mix

1½ cups milk

1 cup mini marshmallows

3 bars (1.55 ounces each) milk chocolate bars, broken into pieces *or* 1 cup milk chocolate chips

3 whole graham crackers, broken into bite-size pieces

**1.** Preheat oven to 350°F. Spray 13×9-inch baking pan with nonstick cooking spray.

**2.** Combine cake mix, pudding mix and milk in large bowl; beat 2 minutes or until well blended. Spread evenly in prepared pan.

**3.** Bake 30 to 35 minutes or until toothpick inserted into center comes out clean. *Turn oven to broil.*

**4.** Sprinkle marshmallows, chocolate and graham crackers over cake. Broil 6 inches from heat source 30 seconds to 1 minute or until marshmallows are golden brown. (Watch carefully to prevent burning.) Cool at least 5 minutes before serving.

# DOUBLE CHOCOLATE BUNDT CAKE

MAKES 10 TO 12 SERVINGS

1 package (about 15 ounces) chocolate cake mix

1 package (4-serving size) chocolate instant pudding and pie filling mix

4 eggs

¾ cup water

¾ cup sour cream

½ cup oil

1 cup semisweet chocolate chips

Powdered sugar

**1.** Preheat oven to 350°F. Spray 10-inch bundt or tube pan with nonstick cooking spray.

**2.** Beat cake mix, pudding mix, eggs, water, sour cream and oil in large bowl with electric mixer at medium speed 2 minutes. Stir in chocolate chips; pour into prepared pan.

**3.** Bake 55 to 60 minutes or until cake springs back when lightly touched. Cool 1 hour in pan on wire rack. Invert cake onto serving plate; cool completely. Sprinkle with powdered sugar before serving.

# ROCKY ROAD CAKE

## MAKES 12 TO 16 SERVINGS

1 package (about 15 ounces) devil's food cake mix

1⅓ cups water

3 eggs

½ cup vegetable oil

2 teaspoons instant coffee granules (optional)

4 cups mini marshmallows

1 cup chopped walnuts or pecans, toasted*

1 container (16 ounces) hot fudge topping, heated according to package directions

*Spread in single layer on baking sheet. Bake in preheated 350°F oven 5 to 7 minutes or until lightly browned, stirring frequently.*

1. Preheat oven to 350°F. Grease 13×9-inch baking pan.

2. Beat cake mix, water, eggs, oil and coffee granules, if desired, in large bowl with electric mixer at low speed 1 minute or until well blended. Pour batter into prepared pan.

3. Bake 30 minutes or until toothpick inserted into center comes out almost clean. Immediately sprinkle marshmallows over cake; top with walnuts. Cool in pan 15 minutes.

4. Drizzle hot fudge topping evenly over cake; cool completely.

# TURTLE DUMP CAKE

MAKES 12 TO 16 SERVINGS

1 package (about 15 ounces) devil's food cake mix

1 package (4-serving size) chocolate instant pudding and pie filling mix

1½ cups milk

1 cup chopped caramels

1 cup semisweet chocolate chips

½ cup pecan pieces

½ teaspoon coarse salt

**1.** Preheat oven to 350°F. Spray 13×9-inch baking pan with nonstick cooking spray.

**2.** Combine cake mix, pudding mix and milk in large bowl; beat 2 minutes or until well blended. Spread evenly in prepared pan; top with caramels, chocolate chips and pecans. Sprinkle with salt, if desired.

**3.** Bake 30 to 35 minutes or until toothpick inserted into center comes out clean. Cool in pan at least 15 minutes before serving.

# COOKIES AND CREAM CAKE

MAKES 10 TO 12 SERVINGS

1 package (about 15 ounces) white cake mix

1 package (4-serving size) white chocolate instant pudding and pie filling mix

1 cup vegetable oil

4 egg whites

½ cup milk

20 chocolate sandwich cookies, coarsely chopped

½ cup semisweet chocolate chips, melted

4 chocolate sandwich cookies, cut into quarters

**1.** Preheat oven to 350°F. Spray 12-cup bundt pan with nonstick cooking spray.

**2.** Beat cake mix, pudding mix, oil, egg whites and milk in large bowl with electric mixer at medium speed 2 minutes or until well blended. Stir in chopped cookies; spread batter in prepared pan.

**3.** Bake 50 to 60 minutes or until cake springs back when lightly touched. Cool 1 hour in pan on wire rack. Invert cake onto serving plate; cool completely. Drizzle with melted chocolate and top with quartered cookies.

# CHOCOLATE MYSTERY CAKE

MAKES 12 TO 16 SERVINGS

1 package (about 15 ounces) German chocolate cake mix

1½ cups plus 2 tablespoons root beer (not diet soda), divided

2 eggs

¼ cup vegetable oil

1 container (about 16 ounces) vanilla frosting

**1.** Preheat oven to 350°F. Coat 13×9-inch baking pan with nonstick cooking spray.

**2.** Combine cake mix, 1½ cups root beer, eggs and oil in large bowl. Beat with electric mixer at low speed 30 seconds. Beat at medium speed 2 minutes or until well blended. Spread batter in prepared pan.

**3.** Bake 30 minutes or until toothpick inserted into center comes out clean. Cool completely in pan on wire rack.

**4.** Whisk remaining 2 tablespoons root beer into frosting until well blended. Spread frosting over cooled cake.

# .CLASSIC.
# DUMP CAKES

# BLACKBERRY ALMOND DUMP CAKE

MAKES 12 TO 16 SERVINGS

2 packages (12 ounces each) frozen blackberries, thawed and drained

¼ cup granulated sugar

1 package (about 15 ounces) yellow cake mix

¾ cup (1½ sticks) butter, cut into thin slices

½ cup sliced almonds

¼ cup packed brown sugar

**1.** Preheat oven to 350°F. Spray 13×9-inch baking pan with nonstick cooking spray.

**2.** Spread blackberries in prepared pan; sprinkle with granulated sugar and toss to coat. Top evenly with cake mix. Top with butter in single layer, covering cake mix as much as possible. Sprinkle with almonds and brown sugar.

**3.** Bake 50 to 60 minutes or until toothpick inserted into center of cake comes out clean. Cool at least 15 minutes before serving.

# Raspberry Lovers' Dump Cake

MAKES 12 TO 16 SERVINGS

1 can (21 ounces) raspberry pie filling

1 package (12 ounces) frozen raspberries, thawed and drained

1 package (12 ounces) semisweet chocolate chips

1 package (about 15 ounces) white cake mix

¾ cup (1½ sticks) butter, cut into thin slices

½ cup packed brown sugar

Ice cream (optional)

**1.** Preheat oven to 350°F. Spray 13×9-inch baking pan with nonstick cooking spray.

**2.** Spread raspberry pie filling in prepared pan; sprinkle with raspberries. Sprinkle with half of chocolate chips. Top with cake mix, spreading evenly. Top with butter in single layer, covering cake mix as much as possible. Sprinkle with brown sugar and remaining chocolate chips.

**3.** Bake 50 to 60 minutes or until golden brown and toothpick inserted into center of cake comes out clean. Cool at least 15 minutes before serving. Serve with ice cream, if desired.

# GRANOLA CARAMEL CARROT DUMP CAKE

MAKES 12 TO 16 SERVINGS

1 can (20 ounces) crushed pineapple, undrained

1 package (about 15 ounces) carrot cake mix

½ cup (1 stick) butter, cut into thin slices

1 cup granola

3 tablespoons caramel topping, warmed

Ice cream (optional)

**1.** Preheat oven to 350°F. Spray 13×9-inch baking pan with nonstick cooking spray.

**2.** Spread pineapple in prepared pan. Top evenly with cake mix. Top with butter in single layer, covering cake mix as much as possible. Sprinkle with granola; drizzle with caramel topping.

**3.** Bake 50 to 55 minutes or until toothpick inserted into center of cake comes out clean. Cool at least 15 minutes before serving. Serve with ice cream, if desired.

# PEACH STRAWBERRY DUMP CAKE

MAKES 12 TO 16 SERVINGS

1   can (29 ounces) peach slices in light syrup, undrained

1½  cups frozen sliced strawberries, thawed and drained

1   package (about 15 ounces) yellow cake mix

½   cup (1 stick) butter, melted

    Ice cream (optional)

**1.** Preheat oven to 350°F. Spray 13×9-inch baking pan with nonstick cooking spray.

**2.** Spread peaches and strawberries in prepared pan. Top with cake mix, spreading evenly. Pour butter over top, covering cake mix as much as possible.

**3.** Bake 50 to 55 minutes or until toothpick inserted into center of cake comes out clean. Cool at least 15 minutes before serving. Serve with ice cream, if desired.

# DOUBLE BANANA
# DUMP CAKE

MAKES 9 SERVINGS

1 package (about 18 ounces) banana cake mix, plus ingredients to prepare mix

¾ cup chopped hazelnuts or sliced almonds, toasted* and divided

1 banana, thinly sliced

4 tablespoons chocolate hazelnut spread, heated**

*To toast hazelnuts, spread in single layer on ungreased baking sheet. Bake in preheated 350°F oven 5 to 7 minutes or until light brown, stirring occasionally.*

**Microwave on LOW (30%) about 1 minute or until pourable.*

**1.** Preheat oven to 350°F. Spray 9-inch square baking pan with nonstick cooking spray.

**2.** Prepare cake mix according to package directions; stir in ½ cup hazelnuts. Spread half of batter in prepared pan. Top with banana slices; drizzle with 2 tablespoons chocolate hazelnut spread. Top with remaining half of batter; sprinkle with remaining ¼ cup hazelnuts and drizzle with remaining 2 tablespoons chocolate hazelnut spread.

**3.** Bake 25 to 30 minutes or until toothpick inserted into center comes out clean. Cool in pan 15 minutes before serving.

# BANANA SPLIT DUMP CAKE

MAKES 12 TO 16 SERVINGS

1 can (20 ounces) crushed pineapple, undrained

1 can (14½ ounces) tart cherries in water, drained

1 package (about 18 ounces) banana cake mix

½ cup (1 stick) butter, cut into thin slices

½ cup semisweet chocolate chips

½ cup chopped pecans

Whipped cream and maraschino cherries (optional)

**1.** Preheat oven to 350°F. Spray 13×9-inch baking pan with nonstick cooking spray.

**2.** Spread pineapple and cherries in prepared pan. Top with cake mix, spreading evenly. Top with butter in single layer, covering cake mix as much as possible. Sprinkle with chocolate chips and pecans.

**3.** Bake 55 to 60 minutes or until toothpick inserted into center of cake comes out clean. Cool at least 15 minutes before serving. Top with whipped cream and cherries, if desired.

# PEACH MELBA DUMP CAKE

MAKES 12 TO 16 SERVINGS

2 cans (21 ounces each) peach pie filling

1 package (12 ounces) frozen raspberries, thawed and drained

1 package (about 15 ounces) yellow cake mix

½ cup (1 stick) butter, cut into thin slices

Ice cream (optional)

**1.** Preheat oven to 350°F. Spray 13×9-inch baking pan with nonstick cooking spray.

**2.** Spread peach pie filling in prepared pan; sprinkle with raspberries. Top evenly with cake mix. Top with butter in single layer, covering cake mix as much as possible.

**3.** Bake 40 to 45 minutes or until toothpick inserted into center of cake comes out clean. Cool at least 15 minutes before serving. Serve with ice cream, if desired.

# CARAMEL APPLE PEANUT DUMP CAKE

## MAKES 12 TO 16 SERVINGS

2 cans (21 ounces each) apple pie filling

½ cup lightly salted peanuts, divided

1 package (about 15 ounces) yellow cake mix

½ cup (1 stick) butter, cut into thin slices

⅓ cup caramel topping, warmed

**1.** Preheat oven to 350°F. Spray 13×9-inch baking pan with nonstick cooking spray.

**2.** Spread apple pie filling in prepared pan; sprinkle with ¼ cup peanuts. Top with cake mix, spreading evenly. Top with butter in single layer, covering cake mix as much as possible. Drizzle with caramel topping; sprinkle with remaining ¼ cup peanuts.

**3.** Bake 35 to 40 minutes or until toothpick inserted into center of cake comes out clean. Cool at least 15 minutes before serving.

# DOUBLE PINEAPPLE
# BERRY DUMP CAKE

MAKES 12 TO 16 SERVINGS

1   can (20 ounces) crushed
    pineapple, undrained

1   package (12 ounces) frozen
    mixed berries, thawed and
    drained

1   package (about 15 ounces)
    pineapple cake mix

½   cup (1 stick) butter, cut into
    thin slices

    Whipped cream (optional)

**1.** Preheat oven to 350°F. Spray 13×9-inch baking pan with nonstick cooking spray.

**2.** Spread pineapple and berries in prepared pan. Top with cake mix, spreading evenly. Top with butter in single layer, covering cake mix as much as possible.

**3.** Bake 45 to 50 minutes or until toothpick inserted into center of cake comes out clean. Cool at least 15 minutes before serving. Serve with whipped cream, if desired.

# SUPER STRAWBERRY DUMP CAKE

MAKES 12 TO 16 SERVINGS

3  cups thawed frozen or fresh strawberries, cut into halves or quarters

1  package (about 15 ounces) strawberry cake mix

½  cup (1 stick) butter, cut into thin slices

Whipped cream (optional)

**1.** Preheat oven to 350°F. Spray 13×9-inch baking pan with nonstick cooking spray.

**2.** Spread strawberries in prepared pan. Top with cake mix, spreading evenly. Top with butter in single layer, covering cake mix as much as possible.

**3.** Bake 45 to 50 minutes or until toothpick inserted into center of cake comes out clean. Cool at least 15 minutes before serving. Serve with whipped cream, if desired.

# PUMPKIN PECAN DUMP CAKE

MAKES 12 TO 16 SERVINGS

1 can (15 ounces) pumpkin puree

1 can (12 ounces) evaporated milk

1 cup packed brown sugar

3 eggs

2 teaspoons pumpkin pie spice

½ teaspoon salt

1 package (about 15 ounces) yellow cake mix

¾ cup (1½ sticks) butter, cut into thin slices

½ cup pecan halves

**1.** Preheat oven to 350°F. Spray 13×9-inch baking pan with nonstick cooking spray.

**2.** Combine pumpkin, evaporated milk, brown sugar, eggs, pumpkin pie spice and salt in medium bowl; stir until well blended. Pour into prepared pan; top with cake mix, spreading evenly. Top with butter in single layer, covering cake mix as much as possible. Sprinkle with pecans.

**3.** Bake about 1 hour or until toothpick inserted into center of cake comes out clean. Cool completely in pan on wire rack.